Introduction

Believe it or not, there has never been a better time to break into freelance writing online. The demand for decent native English writers has never been higher – and you don't need a PhD or even a college education to jump into the market.

To many people, the idea of working for themselves and making a full time living by writing online might seem mysterious, difficult, or far away. The fact is none of these descriptions have to be true. This guide will help show you how many amazing opportunities you have to make a full time living as a freelance writer from the comfort of your own home, and just how quickly your life can change once you commit yourself to this path.

The rapid rise of technology, especially that of the Internet, has led to incredible changes over the past decade or so. While many may mourn how print markets are "dying" or how things are changing – online freelance writing gives more opportunities than ever before. If you can write at even a consistent junior high level of American English and are willing to put in the effort to find work then you might be amazed how quickly you can build a successful freelance writing business.

Now I'm not going to lie to you – it will take work and in the beginning you could be working a lot more than 40 hours a week to get going. But once you put in that work, it can keep paying off again and again down the line. Think of how your life would change if you could make thousands and thousands of dollars a month from home... or from anywhere you had an Internet connection. The travel and lifestyle possibilities you would have can boggle the mind.

This isn't a faraway dream... it's a business reality that YOU can create for yourself.

There are a lot of books and e-books online promising how to teach you to make money freelancing online, but you'll find a lot of them are heavy on fluff and generalizations and weak on the actual meat. You'll find that this book does NOT fall into that category because I have created it to be as useful as possible for all levels of beginning writers.

What makes this book different?

So, what will set this book apart from all the other books or online courses you have purchased that just haven't delivered? Quite a bit, actually. One of the first things you might notice is that this particular book is much shorter than many other freelancing books out there. Why is this?

FREELANCE WRITING BOOTCAMP

Caleb Krieger

GetBootcampBooks.com

Published by Bootcamp Books

Read. Learn. Take action.

GetBootcampBooks.com

ISBN: 0615790240
ISBN-13: 978-0615790244

CONTENTS

The reasons are simple. I don't believe in excess words and useless fluff. I'm not here to give you 5 pages of good information wrapped up in 95 pages of useless generalizations. I want everything I write to be useful, informative and most importantly actionable.

You should be able to read any page of this book and immediately have information you can put into ACTION to get your freelance writing career launching off the ground. Most people want the income and freedom that comes from an online freelance writing career, they may even take the steps to read some books on the subject, but too many times they will not take the necessary action needed to make this a career.

The philosophy behind Bootcamp Books is that you are in basic training. My goal, as your instructor, is to equip you with the necessary tools so that when you are on the battlefield, you will know what to do. Often times, people make the mistake of becoming lifelong learners of a subject. While continuing to learn a business or a skill is definitely an important piece of the puzzle, at some point you need to graduate your training and start implementing the training by taking action in the real world.

Importance of taking action
One of the first things that needs to be emphasized is the importance of taking action. If you ask successful and established freelance writers what their best advice for beginners is, you'll hear some version of the same answer come up again and again: "Don't hesitate – just get started." This cannot be

emphasized enough. It's not even a side note, it's the single most important piece of advice you can follow to make money freelance writing online. Seriously, get started now! Take action!

Like in so many other businesses, there is a process of learning the ins and outs of freelance writing online as well as discovering what works best for you. This type of information cannot be taught to you in a book; sometimes, it can only come from experience. Everybody is going to make mistakes and whenever you try something new (like online freelance writing) you are going to make some mistakes along the way and you will have growing pains.

This is actually great news! Don't be discouraged by mistakes – embrace them as the learning experiences that they are. The more mistakes you have, the better you will get at giving customers what they want the first time, delivering work that gets you raises and that builds your reputation and the better you will become as a writer and freelance writing business owner.

The sooner you start, the sooner you'll grow. This book is designed to guide you to creating a strong and sustainable online freelance writing income as quickly as possible. The information I give you is as brief as possible, geared towards direct action and designed to get you moving as quickly as possible to help you establish your own online freelance writing career.

So grab a cup of coffee or your favorite drink and let's get moving with the first steps towards your new career and the new life it can bring!

Chapter 1

Getting Started

While I want to dive right into the specific sites that have worked best for me online, as well as the later section on finding private clients, there are some things you need to be aware of before jumping into the world of freelance writing. Take these skills and attitudes to heart and you will be on your way to becoming a successful freelance writer.

Are you prepared for the freelancer's life?

While there are definitely some great benefits of living the freelance writer's lifestyle, you are going to also experience many problems, frustrations and hardships that no one warns you about. If you are not confrontational, you are going to have to learn to stand up for yourself if and when you deal with clients on various websites or your own private clients. You have to be able to fight through lethargy and you have to be self-motivated. There are a lot of these types of mindsets and attitudes that are necessary to have if you want to have a successful freelance writing business, but many books on the subject don't even address some of these basics. The following section features 14 extremely important tips which cover all of the important basics and will get you ready to take on the world of freelance writing online.

#1 - Grow Thick Skin

It's unfortunate that you will need to grow thick skin but it is definitely necessary. You may encounter family members snickering at you and your "freelance writing phase", you will definitely have to deal with problem employers who want everything revised ten times while calling you every name in the book or even deal with situations where instructions are so vague you just can't get what the client wants. Rejection is also a constant in any writer's life. Learn to grow thick skin and never take any of it personally or you will not last in this business. Now that you know you can expect such issues, you will not be surprised when it happens... and if you take action to create a freelance writing business, these things will happen.

#2 - Realize That Sometimes You May Have To Bend Over Backwards

Some customers simply do not know how to do business civilly. Sometimes, especially early on, you will have to do a crazy amount of work and re-working to get the project done as needed to get paid. There will be many times that you realize part way through that you are in the middle of a disaster of a job. In this case, the best thing that you can do is provide unbelievable customer service, finish the job and just politely refuse any future work from this client (or ask for a giant raise that makes dealing with this person worth your time… there's more on how to do that later!).

#3 - Prepare To Deal With Loneliness

Even if you are used to keeping to yourself, freelance writing is a very lonely endeavor. You will have very little, if any, actual face-to-face interaction with anyone while working. You will have family that doesn't quite understand your goals as a freelance writer. You will be doing a lot of writing (who would have thought?) and for the most part, writing is a solitary endeavor. One way to get through the lonely times is to join a writer forum, so that you can at least interact with people who understand you. Some of them may even be able to give you some good advice. While it is important to work hard in this business to reach your goals, you do need to step away from the computer sometimes and enjoy the people and things around you that have nothing at all to do with writing.

#4 - Civility And Basic Politeness Matter, Even When Clients Do Not Reciprocate

It's just simply unbelievable how many would-be beginning writers are straight out rude, never say thanks for any work they get and just make themselves headaches to the employer. Basic business politeness and manners go a long way, even with clients who you want to strangle with both hands. Do your best to conduct yourself with basic manners. When you are separated by a computer screen and possibly many thousands of miles, it is easy to respond to clients in a way that is not polite. Work hard to set a good reputation for yourself and your business, even when customers are difficult, and it will definitely set you apart from the rest, and lead to more freelance writing opportunities.

#5 - Never Be Afraid To Ask For A Raise

If you are a good enough writer for them to want to re-hire you for additional writing projects, then do not be afraid to ask for a raise. Most employers would rather have a steady writer they can trust to do a job properly, even if it means paying more than they want to, than to be constantly looking for lower priced writers and not knowing what they are going to get. While it goes against what you would expect to happen, my personal experience actually shows that by charging more money, I got more work than I do by charging cheaper prices. Plus, I usually have a much more steady group of clients, making it easier since I don't need to promote my business as much, and I understand the clients' needs better since I have worked with them on a number of projects, not just one-off jobs.

#6 - Don't Be Afraid To Drop A Headache Client

If you are having to deal with a client who is causing you a lot of stress and issues, then sometimes it's not worth the time, stress, or effort. While still being polite, you can simply drop a client if it is a bad situation. Do not allow yourself to get stuck in a bad situation. Explain to the client that you are no longer able to work on the project for them, and then you can use that additional time to find jobs and clients that will not cause you a bunch of stress. If it is something you can work through, it is always best to try to finish the job. Sometimes though, dropping the client and taking a loss on the work already performed is best for you all around.

#7 - Have Unshakable Self-Confidence That Is Bordering On Ego

No matter how rough things get, you need to be confident about your abilities as a writer. By all means, learn new skills and practice writing to keep yourself sharp, but always have the confidence that you can thrive as a writer and that you are better than most of your competition. That confidence comes through in the writing and in your bidding for work. Do not be arrogant to clients, but definitely make sure to convey your self-confidence. This will give you an advantage over your competition.

#8 - Opening A PayPal Account Is A Must

This is simple. If you are going to write online, you absolutely must have a working PayPal account connected to your checking account. It's easy to sign up for and most online writing sites pay you through PayPal so you are metaphorically cutting off your arms and legs if you are not allowing yourself to work for all of the sites that pay by PayPal. Yes, PayPal has fees but that is the cost of doing business. You can charge more to offset the PayPal fees. Plus, PayPal fees can be tax deductible (check with your local tax professional) since it is a business expense. PayPal is much safer than relying on receiving a check from a client and much safer for the client as well. A PayPal account is definitely a must-have for any freelance writer online.

#9 - Have Reasonable Expectations When You Start as a Freelance Writer

There are some sites that allow you to make money relatively quickly starting out, but if you just got laid off and you are trying to make money right now to pay your bills this month, that is not realistic. I can show you sites that get you bringing in some money early on but you are not going to start from nothing and start making $500 a week. That is just not realistic and it's not practical, despite what the latest and greatest scam tries to tell you. If you work really hard and apply the information found in this guide then it won't take long for you to start bringing in an extra thousand or two a month, then a lot more. There are more online opportunities than ever before if you're willing to grab them – but just know, it will take a little bit of time to reach that level.

#10 - Prepare For Erratic Cash Flow

Sometimes you are going to have a lot of time between paychecks. You need to be able to budget properly and ride out the stress of infrequent cash flow. Part of the reason I like having so many different sources of income is that it builds a steady cash flow. Some online sites pay after assignment, while other employers pay once or twice per week, once per month or only after a certain earning amount is reached. It's a little bit easier to manage a budget when you have so many payments coming in because you know some cash flow will come in every week – but once again don't sacrifice larger cash amounts or per hour pay for cash flow purposes. It's a balancing act. You need to also be prepared for how the outside world views your income. If you are looking to rent a house, buy a car, take out a loan, or even buy a house, you are going to need to prove your income in a much different way than you would with a regular job. Often times, lending agencies require 2-3 years of self-employment income in order to approve your loan or rental application.

#11 - Definitely Make A Plan, But Remember That Planning Isn't Work

This is an EXTREMELY important concept that you must grasp. If you want to utilize your time well and succeed at making the most out of your online freelance writing career you will want to create clear and concise courses of action to help you to reach your desired level of income. This includes monthly goals, weekly to do lists, and breaking those down into daily "must do" lists. You will become better at this as you progress. While these planning steps, educating yourself and learning more about the freelance business are all important for your business, they not work, and work is what pays the bills.

PLANNING is NOT work.
READING BLOGS is NOT work.
DOING RESEARCH is NOT work.

All three of these steps are necessary in a freelance writing career, but they're also the easiest ways you can trick yourself into "working" 8 hours in a day when in fact you did not get any actual work done.

Remember: you do not get paid for day dreaming or planning, no matter how important they are to running a successful business.

#12 - Set Up Your Own Personal Work Space

This might sound like excess or an optional step but it really is a lot more important than you might think. While it's true you can work from anywhere like a local coffee shop or the public library, or really, anywhere with a public Wi-Fi signal – you will be amazed at the difference in the work per hour you can produce and get done when you have a designated work space that is used for that and nothing else. Make it simple but personal. Some people like their workspace to be relatively plain with minimal distractions, while others want inspirational quotes, a calendar or appointment book, plants, or a more "friendly" set up. You are going to know your style and preference better than anyone else, but try your best to set up your own personal office or work space and get into the habit of only using that area for your online freelance writing work. The other tip is to keep this area clean: studies have shown again and again that productivity goes up and stress goes down in a clean environment while stress goes up and productivity goes down in a messy environment.

#13 - Self-Motivation is Key

One of the most difficult yet most important parts of being an online freelance writer, especially if you have never been a small business owner before, is the self-motivation side of things. You don't have a supervisor or boss looking over your shoulder and making sure that things get done. You're the only one who can keep yourself on task and that can be harder than it sounds. You always want to make deadlines and keep at the process of finding new clients, finding new work, and getting through the work that is already stacked up. Don't overestimate your ability to hammer through a grueling day or underestimate your ability to procrastinate too long – build up the practice of productive habits and self-motivation. You will never be hurt by developing these good habits. One of the dangers of working online is the myriad of distractions. News sites, blogs, YouTube, forums and social networks can all be detrimental to your business if you get caught up spending time surfing instead of working on your business.

#14 - Protecting Your Work Time

Finally, we get to the topic of protecting your time. This might be a surprise for many people, but the view many others (including family and friends) have of freelance writers is that they have tons of "free time" and should always have time to do chores, help out with errands, or volunteer to help for any and all projects that friends and family are involved in. In short: there's a weird feeling when you're self-employed as a freelance writer online that you have free time and you should be available, since you "don't have a real job". People won't respect your time – so you have to protect it. If you don't, you will find yourself working from 10 p.m. to 6 a.m. every morning, not getting enough done, and having people call you wanting more and more of your time. Protect your time early – it will save you a lot of headaches later on.

These essential tips range from attitudes, to mindsets, to habits and to environmental and relational factors that all play a part in your business. By neglecting to take care of any of these things, you will find yourself struggling in your business, wanting to give up. Take these principles to heart, apply them in your business, and you will be ready to start finding work as a beginning freelance writer.

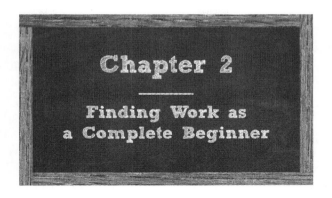

Chapter 2

Finding Work as a Complete Beginner

One of the biggest questions that comes from beginners in this field is how to find work. This makes sense since you are not going to make money if you can't find clients. The good news is that when it comes to the online writing world you have an enormous amount of options for finding work – and even beginners have places where they can go to find work in abundance. One of the biggest benefits of starting your career as an online freelance writer is that you are jumping into a field that only continues to grow in demand. This chapter is going to go over both major techniques for finding online writing work: writing for sites online and finding your own clients online.

Do not be intimidated: both methods are easier than they sound!

Writing for Websites
There are many different websites online that writers can use to make money, but the styles and strategies for getting the most out of each site can vary quite a

bit. A site that seems like a gold mine for one writer might just not be a good fit for another. While it is possible to make a full time living on some of these sites without any other help, many writers find the fastest and most efficient way is to use a combination of these sites. This strategy allows them to reap the combined benefits of frequent payments along with highest income per hour production. Depending on how badly you need to quickly build up an income, how much you need to get by (and how much you need to thrive), as well as what your top priorities are, there are several ways to go about setting up your daily, weekly, and even monthly work schedules.

But to be able to design the best work schedule and get the most out of any given schedule, you will first need to know what resources you have available to you both online & offline and how to take advantage of each. First, let's go over some of the different types of websites available to writers online, then I will discuss other tips for finding your own clients.

Types of Sites

There are different types of websites online that all cater to freelance writers and which are constantly looking for, sometimes even actively recruiting, new writers to add to their stable of paid writers. While not every online opportunity is going to cleanly fit into one of these website types, you can break most websites down into four categories:

- Pay per article,
- Auction/bidding-based,
- On speculation,
- Residual.

Pay Per Article & Content Mills

These types of websites pay in a way that will be familiar to most writers or even workers in general. Websites that are set up in a content mill format pay on a per-article basis. An example of this is: you write one article and you will get paid $x. Some online content mills will have varying rates per article, commonly ranging from $3 for a quick article to $20 or more for a specialty article. They are usually not the highest paying work but the higher end online content mills can be very profitable for writers who can adapt to what each site is looking for and mass produce the required articles. While these sites do not pay as much, you do save time by not having to find writing jobs since the website is actively trying to get more people to submit writing jobs.

Often times, the jobs are up for grabs to whoever claims the job first. With such sites, if you can do well on a consistent basis, you can move up and have access to better paying jobs. You still have to claim the jobs before other writers, but you will have access to those better paying articles, which not as many writers have access to.

Auction/Bidding-Based Websites

While there are a huge number of auction-based websites out there for finding freelance work through a bidding system, four stand out heads and shoulders above the rest, as I write this: Guru.com, Elance.com, oDesk.com and Rentacoder.com are all the top dogs for this type of auction/bidding-based site.

Each of these sites has its specific quirks. These sites are some of the best places where beginners can start their writing career. In an auction setting, employers put up postings of the work that they want done and the freelance writers who want to do the work give their sales pitch to the employer along with their bid for the project. The employer then chooses one or several authors to complete the job for the agreed upon price, with the website often serving as escrow to protect both the employer as well as the hired writers. Many freelance writers make a full time living just off one or two auction sites and nothing else.

While each site will be different, there are some common strategies that can help you thrive when drumming up business from this type of website. One of the best pieces of advice I can give should be obvious: have writing samples on hand. Employers are always looking for more good writers to produce content for them. I'm not going to lie – it's much easier to get work once you have several positive reviews on each site, however many employers are willing to hire brand new writers based on very good writing samples.

For your samples, don't just rip off 100 words on a topic; take the time to write multiple articles on several topics. After doing great research and writing some of your best articles you will want to come back in a few hours and edit and review all of your writing samples. Then come back again the next day and re-write the articles again: you want these samples to be the absolute best work that you can put out. This is your way of making a GREAT impression with employers who are willing to give new writers a chance.

You also want to be sure to maximize your profile on any of these sites. Include a professional photo (and smile – photos of people smiling have been shown to inspire trust as well as create a positive reaction from viewers), your writing resume including any qualifications and previous gigs as a writer, your education information or a history of writing offline. Update your profile as your freelance writing career builds and grows. Employers tend to look at writer profiles and you do not want anything to disqualify you – make every tool at your disposal work for you to find more clients and more work.

Finally, be smart in how you use your "canned quotes." Too many freelancers create a single "one size fits all" type of bid for a project and just shoot them all out. Yes this is a faster approach, but you will not get many responses this way. It is very easy for a potential employer to recognize a canned response or template response versus one that is actually specifically written towards an individual job posting.

There is nothing wrong with having a basic template – but you should use that only as a starting point and never as the final bid to a project. You will get a lot more work by crafting each and every bid based around the job description that is provided. Mention specifics of the job posting in your bid – show you actually read the job and understand it. If you are really excited about the writing job, craft a writing sample on the same subject or topic to include with your bid. Show them why you are the one for the job!

These are little things – but well over 90% of freelance writers online don't even bother. These little things go a long way to getting huge results. If you want to build a very successful online freelancing business, you want to pay attention to these small details. Do that, get a few top notch reviews (and over-deliver big time on those early jobs to make sure you get those top notch ratings and reviews), and soon there will be so many jobs coming in you won't be able to handle them all (which is a good problem to have). That is when you really jack up your prices – and you might be surprised how often you can get employers to pay top dollar for your work as long as you take care of them.

Open Market or "On Spec"

This format isn't nearly as common, and in fact as of this writing there is only one really website that falls under this category and that is Constant-Content. That is not to say more will not emerge in the future as this is a format that can work, but for now Constant-Content is it. For the on spec type of sites, the website hosts a copy of your article, lets you set the prices and terms, but there is no guarantee of a sale.

They attract buyers with a high profile website and when a buyer likes your article, they can buy it for the set price and the hosting website gets a % cut of whatever the article sells for. This allows you the freedom of writing whatever and whenever you feel like, but it also comes with the restriction of not being able to plan for steady income as no sale is promised. It's a catch-22 and the lack of guaranteed pay is a major reason why this format has not taken off as much in the online world.

If this type of writing interests you, browse around the site and see what types of articles and topics are selling the best. Then, if you think that you can write articles about those topics, why not give it a shot. Upload some articles to the site, set some competitive prices, and then go work on other writing projects or attracting more clients. You may just get some surprise income when someone buys an article from you off of one of these types of "on spec" content websites.

Online Residual Income Writing

This type of writing is often referred to as "internet marketing" by many individuals online and refers to any type of writing where payment is received continuously for work, usually in a split advertising deal or pay per view basis. An example of residual income writing from the real world would be book royalties. Famous authors like Stephen King continue to receive payment in the form of royalties for books sold or movies shown on cable that were completed years or even decades before.

Online residual income can come in the form of sharing AdSense revenue earned for your article or on a pay per view basis with payment based on number of visitors to your articles. These types of websites are more similar to the on-spec type of websites talked about above. You are not guaranteed income via these types of sites. Instead, you will be able to earn income depending on the popularity of your content, or receive a share of the profit that your content earns for the website.

As a beginning freelance writer, I would not invest heavily in this sort of writing. Focus on attracting a client base first via some of the other methods mentioned and via the tips still to come in this book. Only use such sites as a way of supplementing your income. The payoff from such sites will not be immediate, so if you need to pay the bills, only focus on such websites when you have a steady stream of clients who are helping to pay your bills.

Starting Your Own Blog/Website

Another way to earn an additional income stream as a freelance writer is to create your own websites and build them using search engine optimization techniques to help your website rank for keywords related to the website. Then, as you get traffic to your website, you can make money a variety of ways, including AdSense, Amazon, Clickbank, or other affiliate networks. This is the method that many freelance writers eventually want to get to, and who can blame them? Who wouldn't want to make $2,000, $5,000, or $10,000 a month every single month for work done months and years ago?

This is a harder road than the other types of places mentioned because it falls a lot less under conventional freelance writing. This route also is not going to pay off right away. There is a lot to learn about search engine optimization (SEO), monetizing websites, and a wide variety of other skills. This is one of those routes that a lot of online freelance writers will choose to do on the side as a long term investment while the more mainstream freelance writing pays the bills while taking up the majority of time and energy. Still, you may consider starting a website or blog that you write on once or twice a week. Not only can you begin to build a following, and even eventually make some money, but what better showcase of your writing for potential clients is there, than your website about something that you are passionate about?

Remember, creating your own website should be viewed as a long-term income source, not an immediate money maker. It is easy to get caught up spending time building a website, tweaking it to make it look perfect, creating content for it, and promoting it. While these things can pay off in the long run, they should not take away from working on and promoting your freelance writing business.

Thinking Outside of the Box
There are other ways of finding clients and often times these methods require thinking outside of the box a little bit. There are a few strategies that I love, that many freelance writers use to pick up higher paying clients. Even if you are a beginner to online freelance writing, these methods below can work for you.

Connect With People on Marketing Forums
One group of people that is always looking for good

content are Internet marketers. The Warrior Forum is probably the most famous of the Internet marketing forums, but there are tons of other forums online for marketers of all kinds. Since Internet marketing requires content to succeed, offering your writing services to marketers can be a very profitable practice. Do some research ahead of time to find out what each board or forum specializes in and have writing samples available on topics that come up consistently in these forums. This little bit of research can go a long way towards getting you some decent freelance work.

Many of these forums have a "service provider" or "services offered" section where you can advertise your rates. This is never a bad idea, but also consider participating in the forums, offering a special per page or per article sale (you would be surprised how many marketers will leap at giving you a chance at $10 a page) to boost your chances of making a sale. Many marketers would like to have a talented and reliable freelance writer at their disposal (and those are hard to come by), so if you can be available, dependable, and if you can provide solid content for them, you will have no trouble finding clients.

Because of this, one of the best approaches to take is to approach interested marketers by mentioning your per page rate as a "beginner's rate." You might feel intimidated charging $8 or $10 a page early on, but call it your sales rate for new clients, win them over, and eventually shoot for $15 a page. When people keep coming back, shoot newer clients a rate of $20 a page and work your way up.

If you are in a "completely broke, bills due yesterday" mode or you are looking at online freelance writing as simply a side income for a once a year vacation or emergency fund then one of the best ways to almost guarantee a rash of sales from Internet marketers is to offer a "one time only" $5 a page deal. You will sell a lot of pages this way if your writing samples show even an average ability to write.

Querying Website Owners

Although I have mentioned it in passing few times, you need to understand one thing about the online world: good content is critical on every level. The goal of many websites or blogs is to rank on the front page of Google. Think about hobbies or interests you have and Google those words. Skip page one and even page two and start looking for websites or pages on page 3 and later. Look for websites or blogs that have inferior content or very little and need more. See if you can find any contact information on any of these websites then contact the owners of these sites and offer to write content for their sites for a premium price. Many won't answer, some will politely decline but others will be looking for high level content and are willing to pay for it. Better yet, if you go to them, not only will they not have to go find you on an auction site or at a content mill, but you will not have to compete with other freelance writers for the job.

This is similar to the old tactic of "cold calling" on the phone and is a great skill to learn regardless because it helps teach you how to pitch yourself – a critical aspect of becoming a successful online freelance writer. This might be a tactic that many beginner writers are nervous about, but learning to market yourself and getting used to the idea of asking clients for work are skills that can mean the difference between success and failure as a freelance writer. These skills will continue to come in handy as an online freelance writer and over time these types of clients can often lead to repeat work or a higher per-page rate than you would generally get off of auction based freelance writing websites.

Connections and Business Expertise

Too often new freelance writers think of connections as only other writers, publishers, or editors. Think about any jobs you have had, fields you have studied in or industries you have worked in. In what areas do they need online content? Where could you use that past experience to provide content in these areas? There are many niches where major online websites hire experts and writers in their fields to help produce more content for their websites. Often times, these are positions that are in high demand, yet there are very few who are qualified. If you can present your prior experience in these fields and if you can showcase your knowledge, you will be able to land gigs that few other freelance writers would be able to.

Don't underestimate what you know. Have you been to college? Dropped out? Graduated? Been married? Have kids? Traveled or hitchhiked? Do you hunt? Fish? Have you worked with lumber, cars, or a wide number of other fields? Whatever your background is, there is fodder there to give yourself an edge or angle into writing online for employers who need your expert content!

26

Many Options Available to You

Whether you go the traditional freelance writing routes of acquiring work via auction-based sites or content mills, or if you step out of the box and hunt down clients via areas you have expertise in that have a need for your expertise, there are many different ways to find clients and to create different income streams.

My suggestion is that you try a few of these methods out. Obviously, depending on how immediate your need for income is, you may want to focus on some methods more than others, but I would definitely try a few different approaches. That way, you will have much better chances at getting both short-term and long-term income streams coming in. Example: If you only focus on content mills, it can be quite a grind pumping out content on random topics all day. But, if you are approaching websites about topics you like while at the same time writing at content mills and putting in bids for work at auction-based sites, you will earn some income immediately, hopefully get a client or two from the sites you have reached out to, as well as get a client or two from the auction-based websites. All of that can add up to a good, solid income from writing.

How you approach it is up to you, your goals and how you want to run your specific freelance writing business. Don't forget, this is a business and you need to treat it as such.

Chapter 3

Running Your Business Like a Business

When you are working to become a successful online freelance writer, it can be easy to miss a simple fact: you are building your own business. Because of the picture of the freelance writer as an independent contractor, the lone gunman of the writing world, it can be easy to forget that to have a successful career, you need to remember you are running a business. Your writing career is your business, and that means the most successful way to maintain a writing business is to run it like one.

Here are some actionable tips that will help you to run your business like a business, even in the face of opposition:

Protecting Your Time
I touched on this one a little bit earlier, but this one is the hardest to do. Your friends and family may think: if you can work at any time of the day and if you set your own hours, why not take three hours out of the middle of the day to help a family member move? How about two hours to go see a niece or nephew

playing high school sports – or an hour for a family get-together afterward? It can be hard to say no to these sorts of things, especially with the freedom of working for yourself. The problem is, if you don't say no to these types of things (which will come up on a regular basis), you will find yourself awake at 10pm with a minimum of six hours of work to do for your early morning deadlines and have none of it done.

When you first begin as a freelance writer, chances are you will have to put in a lot more than a 40 hour work week to really get rolling. When you get work, it still has to be done by deadline. A freelance writing career is just as important as any other job but not everyone will see it that way. Without an office to go to or a boss, you are the only one who can protect your work time and you should do so without apology. Learn to say no to people, even family members. By all means, move around your schedule to enjoy more of life, but there is no reason you should be losing sleep and your precious working hours because other people are claiming your time.
On the flip side, make sure you are not slacking during your work hours. If you are, people are more likely to interrupt and expect you to help during your work hours, if they do not see you actually working.

Welcome to Quarterly Taxes (Oh, joy!)
While this is not necessarily a big thing your first year since you are establishing your business and figuring out what your average income is going to be freelance writing, you will want to keep in mind that you will pay a higher tax rate as a freelance writer because you have to cover all of your Social Security and FICA

taxes (in the US). Traditionally, your employer covers half but as a self-employed freelancer that income is your responsibility.

Freelancers pay quarterly taxes, meaning you make four payments in a year as opposed to everything being due on April 15th. While entire books are written on the topic, the IRS website actually explains how quarterly taxes work very well. You need to estimate how much you will make in a year, figure out the tax rate, and then pay a quarter of that amount on each due date. This requires some skillful budgeting, or you can always use an accountant if you do not want to mess with doing this on your own.

The above is simply helpful information and should not be construed as advice. As each locale is different, be sure to talk to a trained tax professional. Just know that after your first year of being a freelance writer, you will be taxed as a real business, which means quarterly taxes.

Mental Stress

Freelancing can be stressful, especially when you are just getting started. Many writers remember their first weeks of looking for work, of spending 40 or 50 hours answering job ads, putting together writing samples, setting up profiles, and then only getting a couple hundred dollars of work to show for it. Here is the good news: the beginning is the hardest part. As you start building a reputation it will become easier and easier to find new work.

In addition, you will also start getting repeat clients. However in the beginning it can really be stressful to put in so much work and feel like you are only getting peanuts back. This is a normal part of the process. The beginning is going to be stressful and if you have never been without a steady paycheck, budgeting can be really hard early on, but it is worth working through. Even being aware that you are going to go from excited to stressed at some point (usually, quiet often), will help you deal with that transition a lot better, than if it hit you by surprise.

Freelance writing does get better (and less stressful) over time, but you want to be prepared for some growing pains and mental stress along the way, especially at the beginning.

Have Faith in Yourself

This can be called confidence or even stubbornness – but early on it can be tempting to throw in the towel and quit, but don't do it! Online freelance writing may take a little bit of time to break into, at least for the larger paying gigs, but any good or even persistent average writer can do it. Having faith in yourself is critical because your own confidence and dedication are going to determine how well you do.

There is no clock to punch into before zoning out for the day, no clearly defined report card or set of guidelines that tell you when you are doing well and when you are not. You have to believe in yourself and be willing to push through the dry spells as well as handle the rushes of abundance. Without this strong belief, you will have a hard time not burning out which will make it tough to push through over the long term.

Have faith that your work is going to pay off. If you are persistent and willing to fully give it a shot then the truth is that it will pay off for you. Who cares if other writers are making more or getting there faster? You never hear about the ones who try then just give up. Focus on your own journey as you build a freelance writing career and do whatever it takes to re-affirm to yourself that you are going to make it as a successful online freelance writer.

Learn To Budget

Don't be insulted by a section on learning to budget, because believe me: it is one thing to do it with a steady weekly or bi-weekly paycheck. It is an entirely different matter when you do not know when you are going to get paid... or how much you will be paid... or if your employer is going to pay promptly or take their sweet time in doing so. One week you may haul in $2,800 – which sounds great until you remember the previous three weeks combined you made $450.

Budgeting with an uneven income can be very difficult, especially early on in your freelance writing career. You may experience a lot of feast or famine patterns when it comes to getting paid and earning money. Over time this income rollercoaster smooths out a little bit as you get more repeat clients and a high enough per page rate that your pay days last you longer and longer. But early on this can be a challenge.

One of the biggest steps to take early on is to cut out all unnecessary expenses. If in doubt, cut it. You have to get good at making dollars stretch in the early going because some weeks you will have an overabundance of cash and payments – but what if after that you have several thin weeks in a row? It can be tempting to reward yourself after that first big week – and by all means you should – but keep it reasonable. Nothing teaches these budgeting skills like experience, but be aware early on of having to go that extra mile of skimping and saving to make sure you have enough to cover your bills during the thin times. Budgeting is one of those skills that will not only serve you in your writing career, but also help in other areas of your life as well.

It's Business Time

If you treat freelance writing like a hobby, you will end up not making as much money as you could make if you run it like a business. Protect your time, work hard, have faith, and learn how to manage your money with high and low income weeks, and you will be well on your way to running a successful freelance writing business. That is, if you are able to avoid some of the common mistakes beginning freelance writers make.

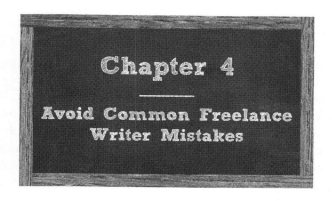

Chapter 4

Avoid Common Freelance Writer Mistakes

Everyone makes mistakes and freelance writers are no different. There are a lot of mistakes you can make along the way as you are establishing your career, but these can also be great learning experiences. That being said, you will want to avoid some of the most common mistakes that many writers make as they are just getting started. These next three mistakes can really hamper you, your business, and your ability to get and retain clients. Be aware of these potential mistakes and try to avoid falling into the same trap.

Mistake #1: Overestimating Your Writing Speed
There are several ways that one can overestimate their own writing speed and this is a particularly bad mistake to make because it can cause you to miss deadlines – which is an absolute killer in this business. Freelance writers in general have a bad reputation for not making deadlines, which makes you all the more valuable to clients if you always hit them or even get done early.

While you want to get a good idea of how much you really can write in a day, you want to keep several things in mind. One is comparing a good day versus a bad day and figuring out what your average is. Some days you will be on fire, others will force you to really labor to get those words on the page. Also do not calculate your average based on a topic you know inside and out. A freelance writer who has been in the business 20 years can write a series of articles about writing without a shred of research and probably slam through them. The same person will take much longer to write the same amount of articles on a technical topic outside his or her field, such as articles on currency trading.

You don't want to overestimate how many pages you can write a day. When you do your averages, do them based on 7 or 8 hours of writing, not 10 or 12 hours, even if you plan to work that much. If you follow this advice you not only benefit from not overworking yourself and making deadlines on time but you also give yourself wriggle room to over-perform and get jobs done ahead of schedule. This allows you the opportunity to make more than you originally estimated as opposed to struggling to hit unrealistic goals.

In the beginning, when you are struggling to get clients and work, thinking about overestimating your writing ability may seem silly, but as you get more and more clients, the more work you will have to get done on time in order to make your deadlines. Missing a deadline can cause your clients to stop ordering from you, so delivering on time is extremely important.

The numbers will change over time: the more you write, the faster you will get but make sure to start that early estimate on the conservative side. You will only benefit by doing it that way.

Mistake #2: Procrastination

This is a huge one. When you do not have a set schedule or set working hours, every morning starts out with a whole day of promise and you feel like you have plenty of time to do anything you want. When you are not used to this type of scheduling freedom (and even when you are) it is very easy to put off getting right to work. The problem is that this forms the habit of procrastination and that will kill your reputation and your online writing business if you do not get it under control.

You might not think of discipline, habits or a schedule as being one of the most important building blocks to an online freelance writing career, but they are. If procrastination becomes a habit, not only will you end up missing deadlines and not be able to get as much daily work done as you need to but you will also be far more stressed out.

Get into the habit of starting work early and hammering it out at the same times every day. This is critical to enjoying all the benefits that a freelance writing lifestyle can provide you. Then, once all of your work is done, you can watch YouTube videos, browse blogs and forums or just relax... only when your work is done.

Mistake #3: Not Charging Enough

At the very beginning you may have to write a few jobs at really low rates like $3-$5 a page. You need to build a reputation, learn the ropes of writing online and get the confidence and experience that comes from several jobs completed well and paid for. However you should not spend a lot of time in this range, especially once you start getting steady work and repeat customers.

Not charging enough happens for a few different reasons. The first is having a hard time figuring out just how much you are worth. A great writer is worth more than an average writer and early on you might not have a clear way of knowing of where you are on that scale. This also comes from simply being afraid to ask for a raise for fear of offending or losing customers.

If you can objectively look at your writing you may have an idea of where you think you are on the spectrum. The other way you find out is simple: you keep asking for raises until no one will give you any more! That's right; the solution to finding out how much you should charge is to keep charging higher rates.

First, understand that writing is a business. Employers, who are usually running a business themselves, understand that you need to make a living. They are looking for a good deal, but they have also run into a lot of dead beats, poor writers or writers who simply did not care about their deadlines. For consistent quality and reliable writers who meet deadlines, employers are more than happy to pay more. If they are not, then you need to replace that client with someone who will pay you what you are worth!

The hard question to answer is when you should start raising prices. There's no clearly set standard on this one, although the general answer is sooner than most beginners are willing. If you find yourself getting a lot of repeat customers, having to work 10 to 12 hours a day or more just on writing, or feeling like you are doing too much work for too little pay – it is time to ask for more money.

Do not be afraid to charge more. Many writers talk about how they were in twice as much demand at $15 or $20 a page than they were at $8 a page. Of course you have to be at least a decent writer and you have to build your reputation to get to this point – but it goes to show that as you get more and more work you should always be trying to push that income ceiling a little higher.

While learning (and avoiding) some of the top mistakes that freelance writers make is important, another important step is sharpening your writing skills. This should be a constant quest for the serious online freelance writer.

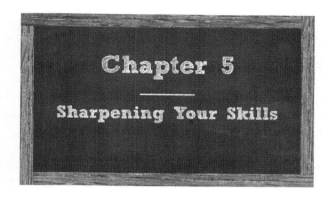

Chapter 5

Sharpening Your Skills

One constant truth of being a writer is that there is always room for improvement. Whether it is learning to write in a new voice for a different market, touching up your grammar usage and punctuation or simply becoming a more engaging and stylish scribe – there is always something that can be improved. Even if you do not notice the difference from day to day, save your first 10 articles, your 200th through 210th, and then take a look once you cross the 1,000 page mark. Believe me – there will be massive differences between these samples and you will be able to notice the difference even if you cannot pinpoint all of the reasons why.

When writing is your career, you should constantly be working to become a better writer. The more versatile you are, the more jobs you can do (therefore, the more money you can make). If you can be versatile and excel in all these different fields of writing then you are only going to make yourself more valuable to new and repeat clients alike.

Even when most of your writing is online for auction sites, becoming one of the noticed "experts" will go a long way to allowing you to keep building your reputation, to getting more work done and most importantly, the ability to charge more. You will want to take an active role in building your reputation and becoming a better writer with each passing day. This is how you improve your writing business.

Here are some tips to help you sharpen your writing skills so that you can become a better freelance writer.

Learn More Styles of Writing
This is one of the best ways to increase your value as an online freelance writer. An informal blog post requires a different voice, style, and type of writing than an online news story or technical content does. Niche content writing requires a different use of skill sets than sales copywriting does. If you only know one or two styles of writing, learn more!

Sales copywriting takes a lot of time to learn and to become good at. This is the writing of sales letters, often for online products. The whole point of a good sales letter is to push the customer towards a sale by pushing an irresistible offer. Good copywriters primarily write online sales letters and can make six or seven figures doing so. It is a good style of writing to learn, and just one example of ways that you can improve your writing skills.

Even if writing sales copy isn't your thing – study the different styles and voices of online websites. Being able to mimic the most common voice or style used in a niche will give you a huge leg up over those competing writers who can't do the same. You can apply for more work, excel at those jobs you do receive, and best of all, you will be able to charge more.

There is nothing wrong with being a niche writer. If you are one of the ten best sales copywriters in the world then you probably should not be wasting your time on anything else considering you would be making thousands of dollars an hour potentially at that point. But most writers are going to always get better by learning different styles, formats, and voices. Some of the tricks and trades you learn from one style of writing may also be what sets you apart in another.

Do Not Stop Practicing

It is also very important not to get complacent with your writing skills. Over time take a look back at your original writing samples and see if you can do even better now. Keep writing, keep working on your craft and keep improving. Do not only work to strengthen your weaknesses but also keep building up your strengths.

If you know there is an area of your writing skills that are weak, you should keep practicing until that weakness is gone. If there is an area you are pretty good at, keep practicing until you excel at that area. This is extra work – but eventually it will pay off with every single article and page that you write. As you will see, finding clients is hard. Your goal should always be to retain clients (as long as they are decent and worth your time), because the less time you need to spend on getting work means the more time you have to write and make money. How will you be able to retain customers? By continually improving your skills so that your clients want to continue paying you to write for them.

Sharpening your writing skills is one of the things that will help you to earn great money as a freelance writer online. Luckily, there are other steps that you can take to boost your freelance writing income to the next level.

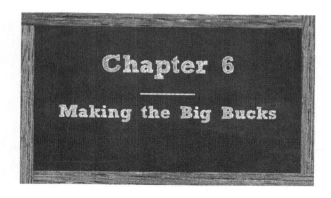

Chapter 6

Making the Big Bucks

No one goes into online freelance writing thinking that they want to stay at $5 a page or make around or below minimum wage. The allure of being able to write online is to get to the point where you are making a full time and comfortable living while having the freedom of time and movement that so many people can only dream of. This is one career where all of those dreams are possible: but that also means learning how to move up the ladder and finding steady clients, negotiating better rates and pay, as well as marketing yourself as being simply one of the best out there.

Here are some tips on how to do all of those things to help you to take your freelance writing income from good to great.

Getting Steady Clients
As I mentioned briefly in the last chapter, client retention is a critical part of any sustainable career as an online freelance writer. While there are always new websites, new writing jobs, new demands for good

words, the key to getting to the upper echelon is to get clients who see your value and are willing to pay premium prices to hire your services again and again. Getting steady clients might sound a little intimidating, but to an extent this will happen naturally over time as you do online freelance work, as long as you deliver good work, on time.

Each hour that you spend trying to find new clients and new work, is 1 hour less that you have of writing, the part of the business that gets money into your bank account. The beauty of having clients that contact you for work, is that you now have another job that did not require you to spend time on marketing. That said, there are some groups of people out there who are always hungry for good writers, so if you do need to find some new clients, here are some of the people you should seek out initially.

Internet marketers are a group always looking for content writers. There are also many companies who need writers but don't want to pay for vacation, 401-k and retirement benefits, taxes, and other expenses that come from hiring someone full time. If you can produce great content on time consistently, they will pay you more to make sure they keep you for future projects again and again and again, because even if they pay you a little bit more, it is still cheaper to hire you, the freelance writer, as they do not have to pay for all of those other benefits that a full time employee would require.

The other aspect to getting steady clients has everything to do with how you build your reputation as a freelance writer. Are you always on or before deadline? Is your writing consistently good from one project to another? Do you communicate during the job and deliver exactly what you promise? Believe it or not, by simply doing your job well as a writer and by doing what you promise, you will stand head and shoulders above the massive pool of freelancers out there.

Reliable and talented freelance writers are very hard to find. You will get repeat work by being both and often times your clients will introduce you to their colleagues. If they know you are going to make them look good, you are going to get more work via recommendations, which is another source of jobs that does not require your time being spent on marketing. Let your writing skills and your professionalism doing the marketing for you.

Negotiating Better Rates

This is a hard part for many online freelance writers, who are worried about scaring away clients or insulting them. Remember what I already told you earlier: your clients are looking for a good deal but they understand you have to make a living too. Either they will pay you an appropriate rate or they won't. If they won't, then you need new clients anyway.

If you find yourself getting a lot of repeat customers, having to work 10 to 12 hours a day or more just on writing, or feeling like you are doing too much work for too little pay then, as I said earlier, it is time to bump up the per page rate. If you are a good writer, your client will be willing to pay you more to keep you. Good, reliable writers are hard to find. I suggest sending an e-mail that is similar to this basic template:

Dear Clients,

I want to thank you all for the work you have provided me. I have thoroughly enjoyed working with all of you and appreciate the fact that you have recognized the quality of my work. The demand for my services is higher than the time I have. I'm going to honor all jobs and contracts currently being worked on, but I want to let you know that as of (date 2 weeks away) I will be raising my rates on all new jobs from (old rate) per page to (new rate at least $3-5 per page more) per page. Thank you all again for your support and I look forward to providing more high quality and money making content for your businesses in the future.

Thanks for your understanding,
Your Name

This is a basic template, but the point is made. You are very polite, no one with a current contract has to worry about prices getting jacked up, but you are introducing the new minimum price everyone will need to pay. If you have a few clients already paying you more than your new minimum price, obviously **don't send this to them**.

Never apologize for moving the basement up. You may even end up surprised. Many writers often find that $15/page writers have more work than $10/page writers, \$20/page writers have more work than \$15/page writers, and \$30/page writers often turn down work because there is just too much demand for their services. Now if you started out at \$5/page, don't jump to \$30/page. That doesn't make any sense. In my experience, bumping up your writing rates by \$5/page increments often works best.

Simple Steps To Put You In The Top 10%

If you are in the top 10% of online freelance writers, you are making very good money. There are several steps you can take to make sure you end up in this elite group and that you are making enough per job or per page that you do not have to work ridiculously long hours to do so (though at times you may have to in order to get there).

Step 1: Under promise and over deliver

This is key. If it takes you 14 days to write an e-book you promised in 10, the employer will be angry and not have a lot of good things to say about your work. If you write the exact same e-book in 14 days after promising to have it done in 21 your employer will rave about what a good job you did and be much more open to giving you a raise. If you are doing article batches of 400 words, do not make every article right around 400 – write 430 or 450 words and keep the charge at where it was for 400. Over deliver and you will take off as an online freelance writer.

Step 2: Always finish before deadline

This is a critical step in the process. So many writers miss deadlines, that it is almost expected – but that does not make it acceptable. By simply getting all the jobs you promised to do by the time they're due you'll stick out from the crowd. That is pretty sad when you think about it, but it is true. Now if you are almost always early, and several days early – then you will have a reputation as an incredible freelancer. All the more reason to always overestimate how long it will take you to get a job done; because that means it is easier to finish ahead of deadline.

Step 3: Open and frequent communication

Clients can be nervous, especially when they are hiring you for the first time or they have a big budget project that MUST be done by deadline. Communicate with your clients as often as possible. Try to never be late but if you are, contact them ahead of time and let them know that you are simply running one or two days behind so they can make plans accordingly. A few updates even along the range of "We are right on schedule!" will make you stick out. I do not recommend saying you are ahead of schedule in case you fall behind.

Step 4: Professionalism

Always act professionally whether it is over an e-mail update, talking on the phone or updating a client on progress. Do not get too cute and do not act like the person is your best buddy: just get the job done and be polite and professional about it. This will also make you stand apart from the competition. Showing an air of professionalism also never hurts when asking for a raise as you give the impression as a business owner who deserves it.

Step 5: Tenacity

Success in online freelance writing takes tenacity. You have to be relentless and continue to pursue new clients, new work, and keep with that faith that you are going to make it. Keep moving the lowest rate you accept higher and higher while always looking for the highest paying jobs you can find – the ones that are worthy of your time.

Step 6: Learn to market yourself

Freelance writing online requires you to market yourself. Think of your reputation as a brand. You want people to think of you as reliable, high end and extremely high quality. You need to learn how to pitch yourself as the best professional available, as the right person for the job. You want to convince potential employers with your words that the only mistake bigger than not hiring you would be hiring you and letting you get away. Setting up a professional website or blog as the base of operations for your business is important if you are going to be trying to attract individual clients. Set up a professional tone from the beginning and your marketing efforts for yourself and your business will be much more effective.

Step 7: Follow the advice in this book

If you are constantly working to market yourself, improve your craft and if you are not afraid to ask for raises, then you will eventually find yourself in the upper echelon of online freelance writers. It's a great place to be, and oh yeah, TAKE ACTION NOW! You have all the information you need here to get started — so why wait? The sooner you get moving, the sooner you get to the level you really truly want.

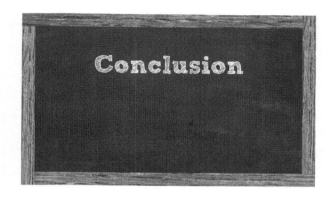

Conclusion

The world of online freelance writing is constantly changing, but that's not always a bad thing. Five years ago websites like HubPages, eHow, and Demand Studios were huge. Now two of those three don't accept writers anymore and the third is struggling as search engines like Google change how they rank websites. Several years ago writers from India and the Philippines were in high demand, but now the demand for native English speaking writers is larger than ever, just a few years later. The online world will continue to change: that's the nature of the Internet, but many things always remain the same.

Quality writers who get jobs done by the set deadline are always going to be in high demand. If you are reliable, that just makes you all the more rare and in demand. No matter how much competition there seems to be, never get discouraged. For whatever reason, 90% of writers always seem to have trouble making deadline and don't act with the level of professionalism you will have mastered if you follow the advice in this book.

Getting started as an online writer is a combination of setting yourself up for success as a small business and being ready for the mental and emotional side of the game. If you are stubborn, dedicated, and you continue to work towards building your freelance writing business you will succeed as an online freelance writer. The print markets might be suffering, but there are just more and more opportunities opening up online for writers as each year passes.

Even though you have the information and tools here in your hands to succeed as an online writer, these are just useless words if you do not take action. The information provided here in this book will remain good even through changing times, so the main variable is you. If you are willing to take action, you will succeed. Do not talk yourself out of starting because you "don't know enough" or "aren't quite ready yet." Jump right in and throw yourself into the work of writing and building your business and you will be amazed a year from now just how far you have come.

But you have to take that first step, those first action steps to get there. You have all the knowledge and support you need from this book to get started but until you are willing to take that first step, nothing will change. Take the leap and a year from now your only regret will be that you did not start sooner!

Write on (and continue reading for our list of freelancing writing websites).

Resources

If you flipped to this page expecting a lot of links, I am sorry to disappoint. I do have a ton of helpful links to share with you, but let me explain to you why they are not in this book, and more importantly, how you can get them.

We live in an exciting and changing world, especially when it comes to being able to broadcast content at such a rapid pace. This fact alone should be very exciting for would be freelance writers because that content has to be written by someone, and that could be you!

Thanks to print-on-demand book publishing as well as ebook publishing, we are able to make changes and those changes are made within 24 hours… for every future copy of those books. Unfortunately, if you own the print copy of this book, there is no way I could update the list of links for you when I find great, new resources or if one of the resources I previously listed is no longer available.

Because I prefer to update you about defunct resources as well as new resources I have found in a faster, guaranteed fashion, Bootcamp Books has setup a mailing list that you can connect with. When you confirm your addition to the mailing list, we will immediately send you the latest, most-up-to-date list of freelance writing resources we have. Then, if we make any additional updates, you will immediately be notified.

While this is not traditional, I think it is best for you, our customer, to have the most up-to-date info.

To sign up to the list and to receive your list of resources, open your computer browser and go to the following link:

http://GetBootcampBooks.com/FLWBC/resources

First, sign up for our mailing list to be notified, and once you confirm your email address, you will be sent to the Freelance Writing Bootcamp resources download page with over 75 websites to help you get started with your freelance writing business!

Thanks for reading Freelance Writing Bootcamp. Now, get your freelance writing business started!

- Caleb Krieger

Other Bootcamp Books

Healthy Living Bootcamp

Declutter Bootcamp

**Come see these and more at:
GetBootcampBooks.com**

12839701R00036

Printed in Great Britain
by Amazon.co.uk, Ltd.,
Marston Gate.